# Marketing
# Public Sector Services

### Second Edition

## Essential Skills for the Public Sector

*HB* PUBLICATIONS

## Jennifer Bean
Lascelles Hussey

# HB PUBLICATIONS
(Incorporated as Givegood Limited)

**Published by**

**HB Publications**
**London, England**

First Published 1997 © HB Publications
Second Edition 2011 © HB Publications

British Library Cataloguing in Publication Data

**ISBN** 978-1- 899448-77-7

For further information see www.hbpublications.com
and www.fci-system.com

# Contents

# Chapter 1

## INTRODUCTION

Marketing is a discipline that is relevant to every type of organisation in both the private and public sectors. Marketing techniques are useful for all managers in developing products and services that meet the needs of their customers, and can assist in creating relevant, value for money public services.

The public sector is a market place in its own right, but the traditional market forces of supply and demand do not always apply. This is because the purchaser of many of these services is not always the end user/beneficiary, unlike the traditional customer supplier relationship which underpins most marketing activities. Hence, marketing public sector services can be more complex and often requires a slightly different approach to that used in the private sector.

There are many marketing books, however, few concentrate on the issues affecting the application of marketing techniques to the public sector. Marketing has become increasingly important where many governments face budget restrictions and there is increased emphasis on demanding value for money. In addition, many public services are now subject to competition from private companies and the non-profit/third sector.

Increasing emphasis has also been placed on user/customer involvement in the development of the service provision.

Many organisations operating in the public sector have to increasingly maximise value for money, by providing the highest quality services within budget limits, which may be decreasing in real terms. Effective marketing can assist in the achievement of this goal by ensuring that products and services are correctly developed to meet the needs of customers and users.

The following chapters explain some of the basic marketing techniques, such as the marketing mix; developing a marketing plan; market research; and so on, emphasising their practical application in the public sector. The text is designed in a manner which allows the reader to easily adapt the ideas presented and apply them to their own work environment.

This book is one of a series of "Essential Skills for the Public Sector" titles. The series aims to assist public sector managers become more efficient and effective in carrying out their important management responsibilities. We consider this book to be an important part of the tool kit for public sector management development.

# Chapter 2

## WHAT IS MARKETING?

Most marketing activities are based on having a clear understanding of what the organisation produces in terms of goods and services and for whom. Marketing therefore focuses on establishing a match between the product/service and the customer.

Marketing should involve the whole organisation, and a truly marketing orientated organisation should identify what the customer wants before it develops the product or service it will provide, rather than persuading customers to take what is currently on offer. This approach is referred to as the **customer-led** approach. In contrast, many public sector organisations are often seen as **product/service-led** due to historic structures, political or legal restrictions, and limitations in flexibility. The two approaches are further explained as follows:

### Service-Led Approach

An organisation adopting this approach concentrates more on the production process rather than on the customer. A great deal of emphasis is placed on the way in which services are delivered, rather than the needs of the end user. This approach usually develops because the organisation has an idea of what the customer wants, or considers that it knows what the customer needs from a professional perspective. The organisation then focuses on the effectiveness and efficiency of service delivery whilst the customer has to adapt to the service on offer. There are many public sector examples of this approach, such as some areas of public health and education services.

It is quite common for the "sales" aspect of this marketing approach to be missed in the provision of public services. This is because the relationship between customer/end-user does not always involve a direct exchange of money (or money equivalent). Many public services involve an indirect exchange as they are financed by way of direct, indirect, or local taxation. This is particularly true of services such as the police, fire, some health organisations and local/regional authorities.

## Customer-Led Approach

With this approach emphasis is placed on what the customer or end user wants or needs. The product or service is then developed to meet those needs. This does not mean that the organisation has to provide an endlessly changing service to meet every desire of every customer. However, it does mean that customer's views are taken into account in the development of, and any major changes to the service.

For example, if a housing organisation were to establish a new housing management office, adopting the customer-led approach, it would first need to consult with the potential users as to location, opening hours, range of services, etc.

In some cases, the public sector is constrained in terms of the services provided and hence may be unable to implement this approach even if this is desired. Constraints may include:

❖ *Legislative restrictions*

❖ *Political philosophies*

❖ *Lack of physical resources*

❖ *Lack of financial resources*

In a market economy where customers are purchasers, they have more influence over the service because they can decide to pay more money for a more satisfying service. However, where services are funded indirectly, it is often not the customer or user who decides how much should be paid for a service. The organisation making this decision may be an appointed or elected representative whose role it is to decide what services will satisfy the needs of the majority of customers/users.

Ideally organisations should aim to be customer-led and should therefore involve customers in the development of services. The following marketing definitions take up this theme of customer involvement.

# *Marketing Definitions*

Set out below are two definitions of marketing:

**"Marketing is the management process responsible for identifying, anticipating and satisfying customer requirements profitably"**
*(Chartered Institute of Marketing)*

**"The action or business of promoting and selling products, including market research and advertising"**
*(The Oxford Dictionary)*

This book will concentrate on the first definition of marketing which refers to marketing as a management process and hence as impacting on all areas of the organisation, as shown in the following diagram:

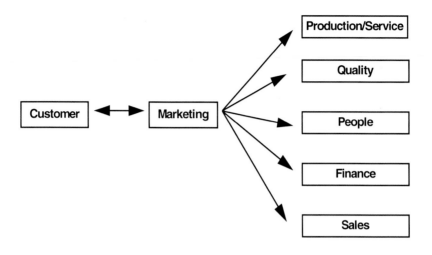

The above diagram shows marketing as being central to the relationship between the organisation and the customer through interaction which involves a two way flow of information. The marketing definition is further explained in the following paragraphs.

## *Identifying Customer Needs*

The most practical way to identify customer needs is to undertake research. Whilst some organisations are unable to fully satisfy customer needs due to constraints such as finance, identifying these needs may still be productive. Finding out what customers require enables an organisation to establish how they should develop in the future, even if resources are constrained and needs cannot be fully met immediately.

Undertaking research into customer requirements follows the same stages required for any kind of market research. These steps are given as follows:

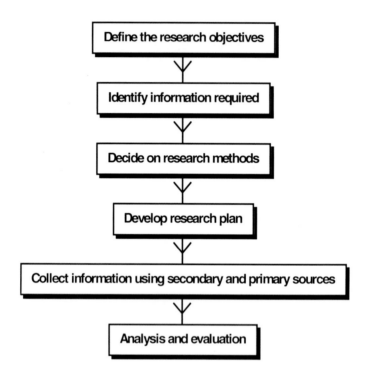

When the research objectives have been defined, the research methods will be determined by the nature of the information required. Research methods tend to fall into two categories:

a)        Primary research
b)        Secondary research

## Primary Research

*Primary research involves the collection of new data, often directly from customers, or intermediaries whereby the researcher tries to learn what customers think about a topic, or how they behave under certain conditions. Primary research is often undertaken where the level of detail achievable from existing secondary research is limited.*

## Secondary Research

*Secondary research, also known as desk research, relates to information that already exists and is available in one form or another. This data may be internal to the organisation emanating from management reports and operating statements. It is desirable to collect data on a regular basis and where possible a database should be established to assist in this process.*

*An additional source of secondary research is external to the organisation. A great deal of this information may be available through government agencies providing statistics and data on areas such as population growth, disposable incomes, economic performance across business sector, and so on. Other published sources are readily available such as research reports, books, journals, newspapers, and on-line from numerous websites. There are also many private sector marketing organisations which specialise in collecting data on specific industries, products and services.*

Many organisations will operate a combination of the two methods.

Shown below is a summary of marketing research methods:

The public sector is increasingly making greater use of tailor made research, however, in order to decide on which research methods to undertake, the following factors should be considered:

a) *Purpose of the research (arising from the objectives), and how the findings are to be used*

b) *Nature of the target audience (how will they respond to questionnaires, different types of media, etc.)*

c) *The importance of the sample size (a small sample can be used in focus groups, but may not be representative)*

d) *Type of information required (quantitative, qualitative, or both)*

e) *Timescale to undertake the research*

f) *Resources available to undertake the work (finance, staff time, technology, etc.)*

Having identified the best method for achieving the research objectives, a research plan can be developed. The research plan will set out the stages and timescales for the work, how it is to be undertaken and the nature of the feedback. This information once gathered can then be analysed, evaluated and used in decision making.

## *Anticipating Customer Needs*

This is one of the most difficult aspects of the marketing process. The anticipation of what customers will require in the future is usually the key to the organisation's long term success. It is clear from many private sector examples, that lack of anticipation can see the demise or reduction of many once strong industry and service sectors.

The need for the public sector to anticipate customer needs is just as crucial. For example, the anticipation of services that will be required by older people in the future. This is particularly relevant as on the whole people are living longer, and medicines which prolong life are improving all the time.

These factors will have an impact on what this group will require from public services, and will affect areas of service provision such as social services, transport, health care, housing, and so on. These public services will need to plan now if they are to provide services which develop with increasing and changing customer requirements.

One of the key challenges to public sector services is not being able to cope effectively with the future demand, leading to a potential break down in service provision. Anticipating customer needs and the changes required for the market place are therefore an essential part of marketing. Such is the importance, it may require organisations to change the way in which they currently operate and may require the introduction of new technologies; the establishment of charges; investment in research; and development of new products and services. This may also necessitate some areas of service becoming redundant.

## *Satisfying Customer Needs*

It is generally recognised that achieving customer satisfaction is an important aspect of marketing and therefore most organisations always strive to do this. The benefits of satisfying customer needs include:

❖ *Reductions in complaints*

❖ *Creation of advocates (people say good things about the service)*

❖ *Reduction in costs (no need to repeat the service)*

❖ *Development of customer loyalty*

❖ *Higher staff morale*

Research can assist in identifying whether or not customers are satisfied and the level of that satisfaction. Increased satisfaction does not necessarily require increased spending. Time spent finding out what the customer/user really appreciates about the service may highlight that simple things make a lot of difference to their perception of the service. For example, a clean and tidy waiting room.

## *Understanding Market Conditions*

So far a great deal of emphasis has been place on the importance of involving the customer/user in the marketing process. However, an organisation will also have to take account of market conditions. As previously stated, market research has an important role to play in finding out about the market place. Therefore, in order to understand market conditions an organisation will need to know about:

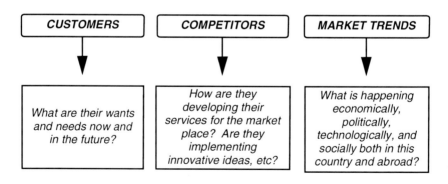

| CUSTOMERS | COMPETITORS | MARKET TRENDS |
|---|---|---|
| *What are their wants and needs now and in the future?* | *How are they developing their services for the market place? Are they implementing innovative ideas, etc?* | *What is happening economically, politically, technologically, and socially both in this country and abroad?* |

It is important that the product or service delivered not only meets customer requirements, but is also competitive and in line with future trends.

## *Marketing versus Selling*

It is important to differentiate marketing from selling as it is quite common for these terms to be used interchangeably. Selling concentrates on the final exchange of a product or service for money (or money equivalent).

In the private sector, the sale usually occurs as a result of effective marketing; i.e. the customer has been convinced that the product or service meets their requirements and is prepared to pay for it.

The sale can be very involved and finalising the sale may require a number of stages to be undertaken such as:

❖ *Submitting a proposal and/or price*

❖ *Negotiating on the price*

❖ *Agreeing the price*

❖ *Obtaining commitment to the exchange, e.g. a signed contract, or a receipt.*

As some areas of the public sector now introduce charges for certain services, selling will need to become a more important part of the overall marketing strategy.

# *Summary*

❑ A truly marketing oriented organisation finds out what customers want before it develops the product or service it will offer

❑ Ideally organisations should aim to be customer led and should therefore involve customers in the development of services

❑ Marketing is central to the relationship between an organisation and it's customers and involves a two way flow of information

❑ Finding out what customers require helps organisations establish how they should develop in the future, even if resources are constrained and needs cannot be fully met immediately

❑ One of the most difficult aspects of marketing is the anticipation of what customers will require in the future

❑ Achieving customer satisfaction is an important aspect of marketing. Some of the benefits of doing this include reductions in complaints, the creation of advocates and reductions in cost

# Exercise 1

## What is marketing?

Given the marketing definition by the Chartered Institute of Marketing set out in Chapter 2, list the activities you undertake for the following:

---

### *Identifying Customer Needs*

---

# *Anticipating Customer Needs*

## *Satisfying Customer Needs*

# Chapter 3

## THE MARKETING MIX

---

### *The Four P's of Marketing*

The marketing mix involves looking at the 4Ps of marketing.
These are:

> **Product** (or service)
> **Price**
> **Promotion**
> **Place**

Each of the above is described in detail in the following
paragraphs. An organisation seeks to optimise its marketing
mix, whereby each of the 4Ps is in harmony with each other.
Ideally, this should be achieved in the most cost effective way
such that it meets the organisation's objectives. For example, in
the private sector, maximising profit is usually the primary
business objective, and the 4Ps are directed at realising this
goal. Public sector organisations may have a range of
objectives, such as maximising service quality.

The marketing mix can be demonstrated by the approach taken
by some tenderers for outsourced public sector services as
follows:

*Assess the needs and desires of the client (Product)*

*Produce the right service to meet the specification (Product)*

*Price the tender taking into account all the factors influencing the price of the service (Price)*

*Ensure that a high quality and cost-effective service can be delivered (Product)*

*Advertise and promote the service effectively to users and other key stakeholders (Promotion)*

*Launch an efficient method to access the services (Place)*

These elements ensure each of the 4Ps are covered with customer focus and an emphasis on service.

Changing the marketing mix is worthwhile if it will result in significant customer benefits, an improvement in the cost effectiveness of supplying these benefits or the elimination of spending on activities that do not produce rewards. Varying the mix in response to changing circumstances is crucial to maintaining the organisation's position in the market place.

Most public sector organisations are normally engaged in the provision of services as opposed to the sale of products. With respect to these services, a fifth 'P', people is often considered. The rationale for the fifth 'P' arises as the organisation's employees constitute as much a part of the "product" from the customer's perception, as any other attribute of the service.

Many public sector organisations will typically place high emphasis on the quality of the actual service or product. In some cases this may be given a higher priority than the other elements of the marketing mix.

## *Product or Service*

The product or service is usually the most fundamental part of the total package offered to the customer. Hence, the marketing objective should be to develop and tailor the service to meet the customer's needs. Issues that therefore require consideration are:

* *Customer benefits*
* *Quality*
* *Inputs to the service*
* *Support services*
* *Client satisfaction/feedback*

## *Product Life Cycle*

The Product Life Cycle is a standard marketing concept which sets out how a product/service evolves over time. This is normally used for the private sector where a new product/service takes time to get off the ground then grows relatively rapidly, after which it settles to a steady level of sales in maturity. If successful, other competitors enter the market place until there is a point of saturation, and then the product moves into a state of decline as new and improved products/services enter the market.

This life cycle is shown by the curve on the following diagram which plots product development in terms of sales revenues over time.

## Product Life Cycle

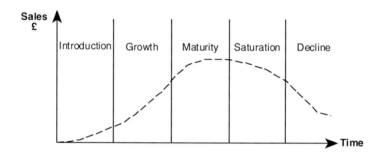

This concept is also useful for many public sector services. This is particularly the case as the market for the delivery of public services becomes more open, with some being delivered by private sector companies. For example, prisons, housing, and health care.

The product life cycle can be adapted for the public sector by comparing the product/service development over time with expenditure instead of sales. For example, the expenditure on a new service often develops slowly by way of an initial pilot project. If successful, demand for the service increases resulting in continued growth in expenditure until a maximum level is reached. This maximum expenditure is usually determined by what the organisation can afford in relation to demand, priorities and other external factors, such as politics, legislation, etc. The service then reaches stagnation as no more funds are available for further development often resulting in eventual decline; either by way of being downsized, outsourced, and /or replaced with other services. This can be shown as follows:

### Product/Service Life Cycle
(Modified for public sector services)

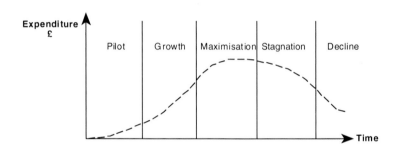

## *Place*

Place is an important element of the marketing mix, as it affects how the customer can gain access to the product/service and how it can be distributed. Accessibility should be continuously monitored to ensure it remains suitable and relevant for the customer. Access goes beyond just physical access but includes access to information and knowledge about the product/service. Issues that require consideration include:

❖ *Customer expectations*

❖ *Is the image right?*

❖ *Using third parties to sell/refer clients*

❖ *Transportation*

❖ *Physical access (disabilities and age groups)*

❖ *Online access (ease of website access and navigation)*

❖ *Style of written material (plain English, different languages, Braille versions, etc.)*

"Place" in the public sector may be a fixed element of the marketing mix, especially in the case of physical location, style of premises, etc.

# *Price*

Price is an important element in the customer's decision to buy, as nearly all customers require value for money. For example, with outsourcing or tendering services, price is often the main determining factor for a successful tender, usually the lowest price. When pricing products or services, there are a wide range of factors that require consideration. These include:

❖ *Cost*

❖ *Discounts/packages*

❖ *Credit terms*

❖ *Payment terms*

❖ *Relationship of cost to price, e.g. profit margin,*
   *subsidies, etc.*

❖ *External factors, such as, market environment,*
   *legislation, etc.*

❖ *Competitors*

❖ *Market prices – supply and demand*

❖ *Client expectations*

## *Promotion*

Promotion can be seen as the whole collection of methods by which the task of providing information can be carried out. It is a process of communicating persuasively and effectively with target customers, the general public, internal audiences such as other departments, and employees who need to understand and support the organisation. Some audiences will require information of a different nature to others and in a different format. There are a range of promotional techniques that can be utilised depending on the original marketing objective. These include:

❖ *Website*

❖ *Advertising*

❖ *Brochures or newsletters*

❖ *Social networking sites*

❖ *Stationery/mailings*

❖ *Displays and notice boards*

❖ *Media (radio, television, etc.)*

❖  *Word of mouth propaganda (positive)*

❖  *Seminars and conferences*

❖  *Public relations*

❖  *Press relations*

If the objective is to obtain more customers, word of mouth propaganda is often seen as the most effective promotional method. However, if the objective is to raise the service profile, public and press relations may achieve better results.

## People (The Fifth 'P')

Marketing starts with the first point of contact between an organisation and the customer. For service organisations, which typify most of the public sector, this is often the organisation's staff. This could occur at any point and with any part of the organisation, therefore, everyone is involved in marketing, even if they are not aware of it. An organisation with a marketing focus will ensure its "people" consider all aspects marketing at every stage of delivering the service, i.e. from the decision making; service inputs and processing; through to service delivery.

The marketing mix should enable an organisation to balance the 4P's to ensure it delivers the right service, in the right place, at the right price and effectively promotes it to the market place.

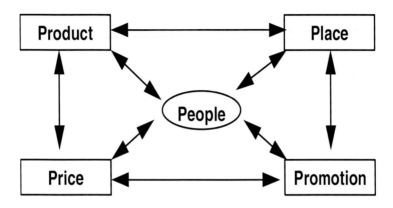

The above diagram shows all aspects of the marketing mix are both dependent on and affected by each other. Hence, a successful marketing mix will not remain static. For example, the product will be affected by customers, changes in the product may affect price and place, and promotion should reflect all the changes that are made at any point in time.

# *Summary*

❑ The four P's of marketing include Product, Price, Promotion and Place

❑ With respect to services, a fifth 'P', "People", is often considered

❑ Varying the marketing mix in response to changing circumstances is crucial to maintaining the organisation's position in the market place

❑ Access to the product/service is important and therefore distribution should be continuously monitored to ensure maximum accessibility

❑ Price is an important element of the customer's decision to buy, as nearly all customers require value for money

❑ Promotion consists of a whole range of methods by which the task of providing information can be carried out. The choice of technique to be adopted will depend on the original marketing objective

❑ Marketing starts with the first point of contact between an organisation and the customer. This could occur at any point and with any part of the organisation, therefore everyone is involved in marketing, even if they are not aware of it

# Exercise 2

## Assessing the Service/Product

The 4P's are an essential aspect of the product/service especially for the public sector. In order to achieve a satisfactory marketing mix, organisations need to be confident they are providing the right product/service for the market place.

*Complete the following questionnaire to assist in assessing your current service. (Tick either yes or no)*

|  |  | Yes | No |
|---|---|:---:|:---:|
| 1. | Do you have a clearly defined service/product? | ☐ | ☐ |
| 2. | Have you set measurable quality standards? | ☐ | ☐ |
| 3. | Are quality standards monitored regularly? | ☐ | ☐ |
| 4. | Are the quality standards publicised? | ☐ | ☐ |
| 5. | Do users understand the benefits provided by the service? | ☐ | ☐ |
| 6. | Are there competitors in the market place? | ☐ | ☐ |
| 7. | Does the service provide competitive advantages? | ☐ | ☐ |
| 8. | Do competitors offer a worse service than yours? | ☐ | ☐ |
| 9. | Do you know how much your service costs? | ☐ | ☐ |

|  | Yes | No |
|---|---|---|
| 10. Are the current costs competitive/ value for money? | ❑ | ❑ |
| 11. Do customers think highly of your services? | ❑ | ❑ |
| 12. Do you obtain feedback about the service on a regular basis? | ❑ | ❑ |
| 13. Do you undertake an annual survey on satisfaction? | ❑ | ❑ |
| 14. Could the service be improved? | ❑ | ❑ |
| 15. Do you improve/develop the service each year? | ❑ | ❑ |
| 16. Do you request suggestions on service development from staff? | ❑ | ❑ |
| 17. Do you request suggestions for service development from users? | ❑ | ❑ |
| 18. Do you implement service development suggestions from third parties? | ❑ | ❑ |
| 19. Are the current users of the service advocates for the service? | ❑ | ❑ |
| 20. Are you satisfied with the service your organisation provides? | ❑ | ❑ |

*For suggested solutions to this exercise see page 122*

# Exercise 3

## Your Product or Service

Where would you place your service in the context of the product life cycle?

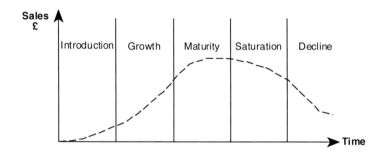

What service development activities are you currently undertaking or do you intend to undertake given where your service currently stands on the above diagram?

...............................................................................

...............................................................................

...............................................................................

...............................................................................

...............................................................................

...............................................................................

...............................................................................

# Exercise 4

## Place

What image does the current service environment give the customer?

| *Describe* |
|---|
| ............................................................................................ |
| ............................................................................................ |
| ............................................................................................ |
| ............................................................................................ |
| ............................................................................................ |
| ............................................................................................ |
| ............................................................................................ |
| ............................................................................................ |
| ............................................................................................ |
| ............................................................................................ |
| ............................................................................................ |

Is this the image you wish to convey?　　*Yes*　　*No*

❏　　❏

## How can the image be improved?

..........................................................................................

..........................................................................................

..........................................................................................

..........................................................................................

..........................................................................................

..........................................................................................

..........................................................................................

..........................................................................................

..........................................................................................

..........................................................................................

..........................................................................................

..........................................................................................

..........................................................................................

..........................................................................................

..........................................................................................

How accessible is the service to all its customers?

---

### *List what steps you take to make it accessible*

........................................................................................

........................................................................................

........................................................................................

........................................................................................

........................................................................................

........................................................................................

........................................................................................

........................................................................................

........................................................................................

........................................................................................

........................................................................................

........................................................................................

........................................................................................

........................................................................................

........................................................................................

## Could access be improved, if so, how?

..............................................................................

..............................................................................

..............................................................................

..............................................................................

..............................................................................

..............................................................................

..............................................................................

..............................................................................

..............................................................................

..............................................................................

..............................................................................

..............................................................................

..............................................................................

..............................................................................

..............................................................................

..............................................................................

# Exercise 5

## Promotion

**Undertake the following steps in order to develop your promotional plan**

| Who do we want to promote to?<br>**AUDIENCE** | What do we want to say to them?<br>**MESSAGE** | What is the most effective channel of communication?<br>**MEDIA** |
|---|---|---|
| | | |
| | | |
| | | |
| | | |
| | | |
| | | |
| | | |
| | | |
| | | |
| | | |
| | | |

| Who do we want to promote to?<br>**AUDIENCE** | What do we want to say to them?<br>MESSAGE | What is the most effective channel of communication?<br>MEDIA |
|---|---|---|
|  |  |  |
|  |  |  |
|  |  |  |
|  |  |  |
|  |  |  |
|  |  |  |
|  |  |  |
|  |  |  |
|  |  |  |
|  |  |  |
|  |  |  |
|  |  |  |
|  |  |  |
|  |  |  |

# Exercise 6

## Developing a Price

If you had to sell your services in a competitive market place, what key factors would you need to take into account in order to develop the price?

- ............................................................................
- ............................................................................
- ............................................................................
- ............................................................................
- ............................................................................
- ............................................................................
- ............................................................................
- ............................................................................
- ............................................................................
- ............................................................................
- ............................................................................
- ............................................................................
- ............................................................................

Using actual figures or estimates, calculate the price of a unit of your service, i.e. rate per hour, rate per visit, rate per application, etc.

|  | Yes | No |
|---|---|---|
| Do you consider this price is competitive/ value for money? | ❏ | ❏ |

> If no, what changes are necessary to achieve a competitive or value for money price, either in terms of reducing price, or improving service?
>
> ......................................................................
> ......................................................................
> ......................................................................
> ......................................................................
> ......................................................................
> ......................................................................
> ......................................................................
> ......................................................................
> ......................................................................
> ......................................................................
> ......................................................................
> ......................................................................
> ......................................................................
> ......................................................................
> ......................................................................
> ......................................................................
> ......................................................................

# Chapter 4

## THE MARKETING PLAN

The marketing plan is an operational tool which assists an organisation to achieve its marketing objectives, through the implementation of a marketing strategy. The marketing plan will set out the detailed steps to be taken over a given time horizon which will act as a monitoring tool for the organisation, with targets and deadlines.

## *The Marketing Planning Process*

The following diagram shows the key stages of the planning process.

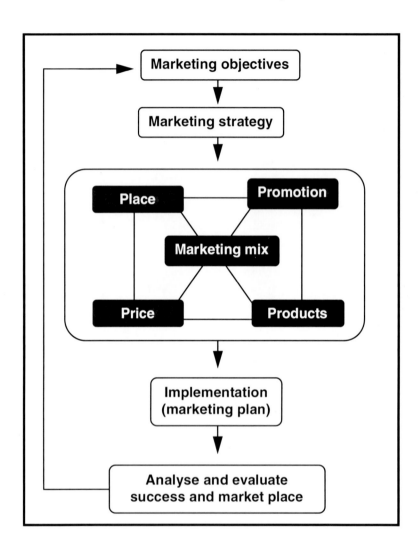

The marketing planning process involves a continuous cycle whereby the results of the plan are fed back into the original objectives. These objectives should be consistent with the corporate, business, or service plan where they exist. The stages in the process include:

- *Setting objectives*
- *Developing the marketing strategy*
- *Analysing the market place*
- *Identifying customer types*
- *Defining target customers*
- *Determining the competitive edge*
- *Developing the marketing plan*
- *Implementing the marketing plan*

These are discussed in the following paragraphs.

## *Setting Objectives*

Objectives should have the following characteristics. They should be:

Specific
Measurable
Achievable
Realistic
Time-related

The objectives that are set with respect to marketing should have all the above features, for example:

1. *To increase customer awareness of the service by 25% within one year*
2. *To raise the profile of the organisation and attract two new funders over the next two years*
3. *To develop a new corporate identity for the organisation within the next six months*

These objectives are clearly specific, and time-related. In the case of 1 it would be measurable if surveys were undertaken before and after the marketing plan had been implemented, and in case 2 and 3, they are measurable by the output.

With respect to whether the objective is achievable and realistic, the organisation has to take account of the resources at its disposal. This usually becomes apparent when the detailed actions required to implement the plan are first developed. If the action plan shows that there is a need for money, personnel, time, etc. which the organisation does not have and cannot obtain, it will be necessary to revise the objectives such that they become achievable and realistic.

## *Developing the Marketing Strategy*

The marketing strategy should form the framework for the action plan, which sets out all the necessary steps to implement the strategy and achieve the objectives.

The marketing strategy takes into account a number of stages as shown in the following diagram:

Each of the above stages is discussed in the following paragraphs.

# *Analysing the Market Place*

All organisations operate within a market place. This could be an internal market, an external market, a local market or an international market. Whatever the market, there will be a relationship between supply and demand. Organisations will provide services in relation to the demand for those services which may come from other organisations or from individual consumers.

When analysing the market place, the following issues should be considered:

### Size of the market
This can be in terms of numbers of customers, financial worth, geographic area, etc. The definition of market size depends on the type of product or service being offered by the organisation. For the public sector, market size is often measured in terms of the number of people within a particular category, such as catchment area, social grouping, etc.

### Competition
Competition in this sense relates to any other organisation which is offering the same or similar service or product. It is important to recognise that competitors do not have to offer an identical product or service. It could be that they are offering a substitute, i.e. it could be a different service but one that would replace the need for your service.

Having identified all the competition, it is important to analyse them in order to assess the impact they have on the market place. This analysis will include looking at the following factors:

· Key products/services offered

- Competitive advantages/dis-advantages
- Percentage share of the market
- The level of threat they represent

## Barriers to entry

Some markets have significant barriers to entry which mean that very few organisations can actually enter. These barriers may include:

- Required level of finance
- Technology
- Scarce knowledge and expertise
- Legislation and regulations
- Customer loyalty (e.g. to a brand name)

Some services provided by the public sector can only be offered by organisations that are authorised to provide the service.

## Market Stability

Some markets are highly volatile and subject to change at very short notice. This volatility can be on either the supply or demand side. An example of supply side volatility is seen in food production, such as crops. The amount of crops produced can vary tremendously from season to season due to factors outside of the supplier's control, for example weather conditions. An example of demand side volatility is seen in the fashion industry where demand is often governed by trends which come and go very quickly over time.

The public sector tends to have relatively stable markets, however, in some areas demand for service outstrips the available supply. In the private sector this disparity would be adjusted through pricing (i.e. higher prices charged for scarce products hence reducing demand). However, many organisations operating in the public sector often have a duty to provide services for groups of people who meet certain qualifying criteria, as opposed to those who have the ability to pay. In such cases, there are few ways in which supply and demand can be brought into equilibrium, the main solution being to increase revenues generally through some form of taxation, or by way of charges to provide more services. Where additional revenues cannot be raised, organisations may be forced to cut or reduce services. For example, less police officers, library services, etc. Not necessarily being able to affect demand via price is a fundamental difference which should be taken into account when analysing the market place for public sector services.

## *Identifying Customer Types*

Having gained an understanding of the market place, an organisation should seek to identify all the potential customers within that market. When this is achieved, the organisation can then, depending on its objectives, target specific customers. To assist in this analysis it is useful to draw a customer/service or product matrix. This matrix lists all the products and services supplied by the organisation against all the current customers/users, some of which may be potential/new customers. It is also useful to rank services and customers in order of priority. This is particularly helpful when resources are limited and decisions need to be made as to which services should continue, and which ones should cease. In some cases, the organisation may also decide which customers/users it no longer wishes to serve.

# Customer Service Matrix

CUSTOMERS

| | 1 | 2 | 3 | 4 | 5 |
|---|---|---|---|---|---|
| 1 | | | | | |
| 2 | | | | | |
| 3 | | | | | |
| 4 | | | | | |
| 5 | | | | | |
| 6 | | | | | |
| 7 | | | | | |
| 8 | | | | | |

SERVICES

| For example: | | | |
|---|---|---|---|
| **Services** | | **Customers** | |
| 1 | Home Care | 1 | Vulnerable Adults |
| 2 | Personal Care | 2 | Disabled |
| 3 | Meals | 3 | Over 85s |
| 4 | Day Centres | 4 | Over 75s |
| 5 | Respite Care | 5 | Over 65s |
| 6 | Residential Care | | |
| 7 | Adaptations | | |
| 8 | Support Services | | |

*The matrix is a flexible and useful tool. For example, inside the grid could either categorise the size of each group receiving the service hence showing the customer distribution across the services (demand), and it could be colour coded to indicate the organisation's priorities in respect of services and customers.*

# *Defining Target Customers*

When all the customer types have been identified, then groups of customers can be targeted. The target groups will usually be determined by the organisation's objectives. For example, a private company that wishes to increase the number of clients may wish to focus on those customers who offer the greatest growth potential in terms of sales and profits. However, in the public sector, the objective may be to target those clients with the greatest need. For example, a social housing organisation will seek to assist those who meet certain criteria such as the homeless, or those in overcrowded living conditions.

It is useful for marketing purposes for an organisation to have the ability to segment its customers into specific target groups. A major part of marketing is communication, and different groups respond better to different modes of communication.

## *Determining the Competitive Edge*

All organisations should seek to have some type of competitive edge over its competitors. An organisation may have one or several areas of competitive advantage that will provide this edge. Some examples of competitive advantages include:

- *Price*
- *Location*
- *Flexibility*
- *Exclusivity*
- *Quality*
- *Image*
- *Size*
- *Monopoly*

In determining the competitive edge, the following factors are relevant:

### Customer recognition
In order for the competitive advantage to be real, it has to be recognised by the customer. For example, the organisation may consider that it provides a better quality service than its competitors, however, this has to be supported by customer feedback.

### Marketing mix
When the organisation has analysed the market place, identified the target customers, and its competitive edge it can use this information to establish the most appropriate marketing mix. The marketing mix is discussed in detail in

chapter 3, with the main emphasis placed on achieving the correct balance between the product, price, place and promotion. The marketing strategy will determine the approach taken to each of these elements. For example, if quality is considered to be an area of competitive advantage, there may be a need to emphasise quality in the organisation's image. This may affect the location of the organisation or the look of the premises; the way in which services are distributed; the approach to promotion; etc.

### Product development

The product or service is a major element of the marketing mix and depending on the strategy to be adopted, there may be a need to develop and change the product. Referring to the marketing definition in Chapter 2, being able to anticipate customer requirements is key to effective marketing. This means that there must be continuous development even if there is not an immediate demand for a new approach. In order to keep up with or ahead of competitors, products and services should be reviewed on a regular basis with a view to improving them in whatever way necessary. Market research will assist in the product development strategy.

# Developing the Marketing Plan

A marketing plan sets out the required actions to achieve marketing objectives which are in line with the overall marketing strategy. The marketing strategy will have determined the target market and how best to use the competitive edge in the marketing mix of product, price, place and promotion such that they are consistent. With this underpinning analysis, the marketing plan will identify the specific steps to be taken along with timescales.

The content of the marketing plan should include the following sections:

## Marketing objectives and targets

The objectives should be SMART in nature with measurable targets. The objectives can be divided into a number of areas, and perhaps the most sensible division would be a split between product, place, price, promotion and perhaps customers. These objectives should then be tied into the detailed action plan which can also be divided along similar lines.

## Market environment

It is useful to have some background to the market place in this document. The marketing plan will normally be used by many people within the organisation, and therefore the market analysis will help the reader to understand the approach that is being taken and the resulting action plan. This information will have been identified when developing the marketing strategy.

Analysis tools such as the SWOT (strengths, weaknesses, opportunities, threats) and STEP (social, technological, economic/environment, political) are very useful as a starting point.

## Marketing strategy

The previous section set out the stages in developing the marketing strategy. The marketing plan should incorporate a summary of the strategy identifying the main strategic areas to be considered. These will include areas such as:

- Target markets and customers
- Areas of competitive advantage to establish the competitive edge
- Key aspects of the marketing mix, e.g. image
- Ongoing service development

This will provide the framework for the action plan.

## Action Plan

This will set out the specific actions that need to be taken to achieve the objectives and meet the targets set. It may be useful to set out the actions in sections relating to the price, product, place, promotion and customers, especially if the objectives have been set out in this way. For example:

---

### *Promotion Objective*

*For the organisation to create a high quality image by the end of the financial year*

---

The promotional action plan may include some of the following:

| ACTION | TIMESCALE | RESPONSIBILITY |
|---|---|---|
| Review corporate literature to ensure it reflects the quality of service accurately, and revise where necessary | By June | A.J. Smith |
| Gain positive press coverage emphasising the quality of the service | Two articles per month | P.O. Cohen |
| Undertake a customer survey to establish an impression of the organisation's quality | By August and 6 months later | R.S. Singh |

This action plan will provide a working document for monitoring purposes.

## Costs

This is an important section of the marketing plan, as many of the actions specified will have cost implications. It is important that if the marketing plan is to be successfully implemented, sufficient resources are provided. This includes finance and personnel. This is particularly crucial if the organisation does not have staff dedicated to marketing activities. Marketing can often take a considerable time and may be difficult to add to someone's existing day to day duties. Some organisations decide to outsource the implementation of their marketing plan, to one or more consultants, professional agencies, or to engage experienced temporary staff. These decisions also have considerable cost implications. It is not unusual to have a PR and/or advertising agency implementing many of the communications activities on the organisation's behalf.

## Implementing the Marketing Plan

Given that a considerable amount of effort is required to produce a comprehensive marketing plan, it is important that the organisation has a clear implementation strategy. This should include the following:

❖ *Commitment from the top of the organisation to ensure that the necessary resources are allocated*

❖ *Regular monitoring of the plan – checking that actions have been performed within the timescale, and where appropriate obtaining explanations as to why they have not been achieved.*

❖ *Ensuring that action is taken where difficulties arise – this may require changing timescales or the personnel responsible for undertaking the activity*

❖ *Altering plans to reflect changes in the environment – this may mean a refocusing or repositioning of the service to keep in line with the competition, or to meet the changing customer requirements*

❖ *Reviewing the entire plan on a regular basis – usually annually, and updating it to reflect new objectives, targets and the changing marketing environment*

# *Summary*

❑   The marketing plan is an operational tool which assists the organisation in the achievement of its marketing objectives, through the implementation of the marketing strategy

❑   As with most planning processes, the marketing planning process involves a continuous cycle whereby the results of the plan are fed back into the organisation's original objectives

❑   Marketing objectives should be SMART (specific, measurable, achievable, realistic and time-related)

❑   Given that a considerable amount of effort is required to produce a comprehensive marketing plan, it is important that the organisation has a clear implementation strategy

# Exercise 7

## Market Analysis

For your service area consider the Strengths and Weaknesses, and the Opportunities and Threats (SWOT) affecting your service in the current market conditions.

### SWOT ANALYSIS

| *STRENGTHS* | *WEAKNESSES* |
|---|---|
| e.g. long standing clients | e.g. Limited marketing budget |
| *OPPORTUNITIES* | *THREATS* |
| e.g. Potential new services | e.g. Loss of funding |

For your service area, consider the Social, Technological, Economic/environment and Political factors (STEP) that may have an impact on your service and the market in which it operates.

## STEP ANALYSIS

| SOCIAL | TECHNOLOGICAL |
|---|---|
| e.g. Increased social mobility | e.g. New ways of working |
| ECONOMIC | POLITICAL |
| e.g. Increased inflation | e.g. New legislation |

## With the information gathered above identify the following:

> ### Areas of competitive advantage
> e.g. price
>
> ..........................................................................................
>
> ..........................................................................................
>
> ..........................................................................................
>
> ..........................................................................................
>
> ..........................................................................................
>
> ..........................................................................................
>
> ..........................................................................................
>
> ..........................................................................................

> ### Areas of competitive disadvantage
> e.g. breadth of service
>
> ..........................................................................................
>
> ..........................................................................................
>
> ..........................................................................................
>
> ..........................................................................................
>
> ..........................................................................................
>
> ..........................................................................................
>
> ..........................................................................................

## *Potential service developments*

e.g. longer opening hours

.......................................................................................

.......................................................................................

.......................................................................................

.......................................................................................

.......................................................................................

.......................................................................................

.......................................................................................

.......................................................................................

## *Potential new markets*

e.g. neighbouring areas

.......................................................................................

.......................................................................................

.......................................................................................

.......................................................................................

.......................................................................................

.......................................................................................

.......................................................................................

.......................................................................................

> ## *Potential for lost services and markets*
> e.g. threats from new entrants to the market
>
> ................................................................................
> ................................................................................
> ................................................................................
> ................................................................................
> ................................................................................
> ................................................................................
> ................................................................................
> ................................................................................

# Exercise 8

## Finding out about the Customer

1.   Describe your customers (list the key features)

- ............................................................
- ............................................................
- ............................................................
- ............................................................
- ............................................................
- ............................................................
- ............................................................
- ............................................................

2.   Why does the customer come to you rather than your competitors?

............................................................
............................................................
............................................................
............................................................
............................................................
............................................................
............................................................
............................................................

3.   With respect to your service or product, what do customers usually want? (List key points)

1 ....................................................................
....................................................................

2 ....................................................................
....................................................................

3 ....................................................................
....................................................................

4 ....................................................................
....................................................................

5 ....................................................................
....................................................................

6 ....................................................................
....................................................................

7 ....................................................................
....................................................................

8 ....................................................................
....................................................................

9 ....................................................................
....................................................................

10 ...................................................................
....................................................................

4. Given the points you have listed in question 3, do you consider your customers receive what they want? If not, why not? (Cross refer to each point made).

**Yes** **No** **Why Not**

1 ☐ ☐ [                    ]

2 ☐ ☐ [                    ]

3 ☐ ☐ [                    ]

4 ☐ ☐ [                    ]

5 ☐ ☐ [                    ]

6 ☐ ☐ [                    ]

7 ☐ ☐ [                    ]

8 ☐ ☐ [                    ]

9 ☐ ☐ [                    ]

10 ☐ ☐ [                    ]

5.　　What do you think is the current level of customer satisfaction?

| | | |
|---|---|---|
| Very satisfied | ☐ | up to 81+ % satisfaction |
| Satisfied | ☐ | up to 61-80% satisfaction |
| Fairly satisfied | ☐ | up to 51-60% satisfaction |
| Not satisfied | ☐ | up to 50% satisfaction |

***This information should be used to help develop your marketing strategy***

# Exercise 9

## Competitors

Using the market place map on the following page, locate your service in the relevant space with respect to price (or cost if you are not yet trading) and quality. The lines represent the average quality and average price of your service in the market.

Next, identify all your competitors and potential competitors, name them, and place them in the relevant positions on the map.

Lastly, identify where you would wish your service to be on the market place map, and then draw a line between where you are now and where you would wish to be.

This analysis enables you to see <u>where you are</u> with respect to your competitors, where you <u>wish to be</u> with respect to your competitors and what needs to change in order to achieve your desired position in the market place. This analysis can then be fed into your marketing strategy.

# Market Place Map

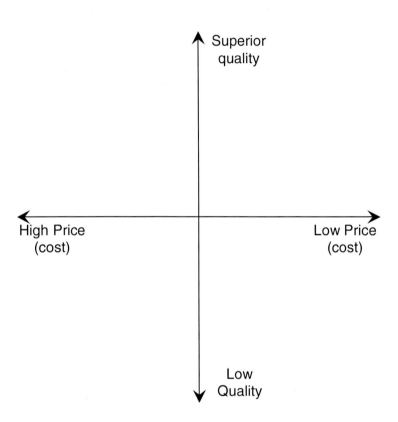

# Chapter 5

## MARKETING IN A PUBLIC SECTOR ENVIRONMENT

### *Differences Between the Private and Public Sector*

Marketing is relevant for all organisations regardless of the sector in which they operate. However, there are a number of differences between the marketing approach to be taken in the private and public sectors. In this section we look at the most common differences between the two sectors.

### The customer

In the private sector the customer is usually clearly defined. It may be an individual, or an organisation which is responsible for the use and purchase of the product or service on offer. This group will be the target for all marketing activities and will be part of the exchange/ transaction process between buyer and seller. In the public sector this may not be the case. Often the user of the service is not responsible for any part of the exchange process, i.e. there is no link between buyer and seller and marketing activities need to reflect this. This relationship stems from the fact that the "public purse" is used to purchase many services on behalf of the public as a whole. This purse is funded through taxes which are paid by the majority of the public. However, it is often difficult to see the direct relationship between the taxes paid and the services received by any one individual. For example, health services are delivered on a basis of "need" and are not dependent on the individual's tax contributions.

In an environment where value for money is a priority, many public sector organisations use the funds under their control to "buy in" or "outsource" services rather than providing them directly. In cases such as these, the providing organisation will have a customer relationship with the purchasing organisation which purchases services on behalf of users. This relationship adds to the complexity of the marketing approach taken by the public sector, in which customers can constitute one or more of the following groups:

❖ *The end user (non payer or payer)*

❖ *The client (where there is a client contractor split)*

❖ *The purchaser (an organisation or section of the organisation)*

## The product/service

The private sector has total control over the type of product or service it decides to offer the market place. If an organisation is customer orientated this will be mainly determined by customer demand. In addition to this, many private sector companies have the ability to adapt their product range relatively quickly to meet changes in demand. In the public sector this is not always the case, as the provision of many services are dictated by legislation, political agendas, the public interest and other issues. The nature of many services, and the way they are financed, also mean that changes can be very difficult and slow to implement. Therefore, even if customer's requirements change this cannot necessarily be immediately matched by a change in service provision.

An example of this can be given in relation to opening hours. In the private sector, shops and offices are often open on Saturdays (even Sundays) to accommodate people who work Monday to Friday, and do not have an opportunity to visit or attend appointments during weekdays. The general public would often like the same amount of access to public services, however, in order to accommodate this need, there may be a requirement to engage more staff and make changes to the way in which the service is delivered. Many organisations recognise that more should be done to take account of customers' requirements, and changes have been made, such as improving accessibility by extending opening hours. For example, many doctor's surgeries are now open on Saturdays and evenings.

**The motivation**

The usual motivation for the majority of private sector activities is profit maximisation. In order to achieve ever increasing profits, there is normally a wish to increase sales, which can be achieved through effective marketing. The investment in marketing can be evaluated in commercial terms by comparing the cost of marketing against the increase in sales revenue and profitability. The private sector may also consider other performance indicators to measure the success of their marketing investment, including:

❖ *Increase in market share*

❖ *Increase in share price*

❖ *Increase in customer awareness*

❖ *Increase in customer loyalty*

❖ *Image and recognition of product/brand*

❖ *Image and recognition of the company*

❖ *Gains in competitive advantage*

❖ *Staff retention and recruitment*

The public sector is on the whole "not-for-profit" and hence marketing success cannot generally be measured in terms of increased revenues and profits as with the private sector. Very often the public sector will be motivated by the desire to:

❖ *Increase user awareness of service provision (what is available and what is not, along with eligibility)*

❖ *Maximise usage of services*

❖ *Reduce waste (e.g. marketing recycling services, or one stop shops to save time in accessing services etc)*

❖ *Demonstrate value for money*

❖ *Educate users*

❖ *Create a positive image of the organisation*

❖ *and so on.*

Both public and private sectors will use marketing techniques to raise their profile, demonstrate quality and gain a positive image in the market place.

## The attitude to promotion

The key difference here between the public and private sectors tends to be the amount of resources available to invest in promotion. Many private sector businesses will find it worthwhile to spend very large sums on promotional activities, as spend can be justified by the returns. The public sector on the other hand is responsible for public funds and large investments in promotion may be seen as a waste of resources that could be spent on direct service delivery. Promotional activities are therefore very often kept to a minimum and have to be justified.

## Pricing

The price of the product or service is a key factor in the marketing strategy for a private sector concern. Some of the factors affecting price include:

### Cost
*Most prices take into account the cost of production, whereby the price is equal to cost plus an element to cover overheads and profits.*

### Supply and demand
*If the market place has a high level of demand but limited suppliers, prices will increase and vice-versa.*

### Research and development
*Some sectors require a considerable amount of research and development expenditure on a regular basis (e.g. pharmaceutical industry) and this cost has to be reflected in the price.*

### Quality
*Price and quality are commonly linked together and quite often higher prices are given to higher quality products. However, what constitutes quality will vary considerably from one organisation to another and therefore the term high quality always needs to be defined.*

### Competitors
*Competitor prices have to be taken into account when setting a price, as the consumer will make comparisons between goods and services and their relative prices.*

In addition to the above, a private company will also need to consider the level of profitability that needs to be achieved. Usually profit margins have to generate a sufficiently high rate of return on capital, otherwise the organisation will invest their resources elsewhere.

Many private sector marketing campaigns concentrate on pricing aspects such as:

Special offers
*"Buy two and get one free"*

Introductory or trial prices
*"First session free"*

Sale prices
*"50% off all goods in the summer sale"*

Discounts
*"10% discount if you use our store card"*

Special terms for payment
*"Buy now with three years to pay"*

A private firm may disregard all logic with respect to price if it can be seen that there is potential for large gains to be made in the long term. For example, a company may promote its product at a price below cost in the knowledge that losses will be made. This is often referred to as a "loss leader" and is usually undertaken to remove competitors or to gain a foothold in a market place. When this has been achieved, it is usual for prices to then be increased.

In the public sector, many services are not charged directly to the public, for example, police, fire, health and education. Consequently, when it comes to marketing to the public, price may not be mentioned at all due to the absence of any price. In some cases price is given a low profile especially when users consider they are paying twice, once through taxation and again at the point of service delivery, such as for aspects of healthcare and education.

Price will, however, increasingly have a role in the marketing of public services, especially where certain activities now have a direct charge attached to them. For example, school meals, home and personal care, specialist refuse collection, dental care, and so on.

## Resources

Many organisations do not operate a dedicated marketing department. This is often due to financial constraints or lack of skilled personnel. Hence, this function in the public sector, often forms part of a "communications" department with a much broader role. This can result in specific marketing activities being undertaken by non-specialist staff with wide ranging duties.

Some areas of the public sector are, however, committing more resources to marketing which is increasingly being regarded as a tool which will enable organisations to:

❖ *Create the right type of public image (e.g. caring, quality orientated, professional)*

❖ *Justify certain decisions (e.g. cuts, closures, reduced services)*

❖ *Promote key social issues (e.g. crime prevention, environmental protection)*

❖ *Raise customer awareness (e.g. promoting new services, encouraging take-up of services)*

❖ *Raise funds (e.g. business and private investment, loans, donations)*

❖ *Encourage volunteering (self help schemes, carers)*

It should be emphasised that any organisation can make costly mistakes with respect to undertaking marketing activities. Many private companies have invested substantial sums on expensive marketing campaigns which yielded very little return. Given this scenario, most public sector organisations tend to be very careful, and generally risk averse, when it comes to allocating resources to marketing. Often the return from marketing expenditure is hard to measure in tangible terms, and therefore demonstrating value for money may be difficult.

## *Developing a Marketing Organisation*

One of the keys to marketing success is the development of a **"marketing organisation"**. This does not mean substantial resources have to be committed to marketing, but it does require the organisation to adopt a particular attitude which ensures marketing plays a key role in all activities.

A marketing organisation has the following attributes:

❖ *Putting the customer first*

❖ *Respecting the customer's wishes at all times*

❖ *Educating customers about the service*

❖ *Developing and enhancing services on a regular basis*

❖ *Ensuring all staff represent the desired image of the organisation*

❖ *Ensuring the organisation's environment reflects the desired image*

❖ *Applying the marketing mix appropriately*

Each of these issues is discussed below:

## Putting the customer first

A marketing organisation will concentrate all its efforts on the customer and become "customer friendly". In order to achieve this, the organisation must develop a customer profile. For many public sector organisations this profile will include:

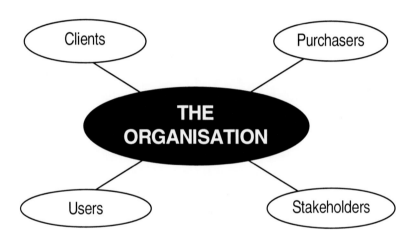

### Clients and Purchasers

In some public sector organisations, service delivery is split between those who deliver the service and those who represent the organisation in the monitoring and control of the service. This split is often achieved by having a "client" and "contractor" relationship or a "purchaser" and "provider" both of which may be contractual. The client or purchaser may be an internal or external customer depending on the organisation's structure. They specify the service they require, often on behalf of other users, and they pay for the service provision. In the usual sense of marketing it would be this group who are the true customers because they are the ones that are paying for the service, either directly or by controlling the budget for the service.

### Users
These people are consumers of the service being delivered, and in the private sector would be the key focus of any marketing campaign as they would normally be the ones paying for it. In the public sector, the user often does not directly purchase the service. For example, we all use police and fire services but do not pay directly for each element of the service; (we pay indirectly through taxation). The user is an important target in the marketing campaign, to influence public opinion or to communicate messages about value for money and service quality.

### Stakeholders
These are parties who have a stake in the service even though they do not directly provide or purchase it. An example of a stakeholder may be a private sector sponsor, who supplies some of the funding for the service, or volunteers who may participate in service delivery, or patrons who lend their name to support the organisation or the service.

## Respecting the customer's wishes at all times

A common phrase often used in marketing is *"the customer is always right"*, because without the customer a business cannot survive. In the public sector this principle is sometimes compromised, because:

❖ *The customer can sometimes be wrong and the organisation always has to adopt what it considers to be the best professional practice whether the customer agrees or not; e.g. child protection*

❖ *Many organisations are providing services for the public benefit which are often restrictive and controlling in nature, where the user may be unhappy with the service, for example, enforcement of parking legislation.*

❖ *In many cases organisations do not depend on individual users for its survival. Such organisations are in place due to legislation, government policies, the public benefit, and so on.*

Going against the philosophy of "the customer is always right", does not necessarily lose customers in the public sector because the organisation in question may be:

❖ *A monopoly provider so the customer has no choice but to accept the service on offer even if it does not fully meet their requirements (e.g. law enforcement services).*

❖ *Offering a free service so the customer has to accept that something is better than nothing, especially if they cannot afford to pay for an equivalent alternative service (e.g. education services).*

❖ *Providing a service to customers which they must have even if they do not want it (e.g. tax collection services).*

Considerable change has taken place with respect to the delivery of many public services such as competition, privatisation, and so on. Therefore, the above points will increasingly be challenged and customer requirements will become more and more important.

## Educating customers about the service

In the public sector, one of the key marketing activities is to educate the public with respect to:

❖ *What is available and what is not?*

❖ *Why certain services have to be delivered in the way they are?*

❖ *Why there is limited choice?*

❖ *What is best for the public interest?*

❖ *What is needed as opposed to wanted?*

❖ *Reasons for reduced or insufficient service provision*

This approach may assist in developing a positive relationship with the customer, such that even if not totally satisfied with a service they will at least appreciate some of the mitigating reasons.

## Developing and enhancing services on a regular basis

Ideally, a marketing organisation should always strive to fully meet customer requirements. However, public sector organisations are not always able to achieve this, typically due to financial constraints. A market oriented organisation can strive towards this goal by continuously reviewing, developing and enhancing services, taking account of customer feedback. This should include their complaints, comments, and suggestions.

This process does not have to be costly as developments and enhancements do not necessarily mean additional expenditure. It may be achieved by changing the way in which services are currently provided, or changing the service completely and replacing it with an alternative.

## Ensuring all staff represent the desired image of the organisation

The most important aspect of the marketing organisation is the culture. This is determined from the very top of the organisation and should be disseminated throughout, so that all staff understand the marketing objectives to be achieved.

For example, if the organisation wishes to be seen as "caring", then staff have to adopt a caring attitude to all aspects of their work. This includes direct, verbal and written communication with the public, but should go beyond this to incorporate:

* *The way in which colleagues relate to each other*
* *The management style*
* *The way in which services are delivered internally and externally*

The image of the organisation can be further reinforced through dress code and general appearance, e.g. a smiling face at the reception desk.

## Ensuring the organisation's environment reflects the desired image

First impressions are the lasting impressions and hence the physical environment has a huge impact on image formation. For example, a tidy clean environment will usually give a visitor an impression of professionalism and an assumption of efficiency. Conversely, an untidy environment may create the opposite effect. It should be emphasised that there may be little correlation between the environment and the actual quality of service delivery, but the public normally perceive such a relationship.

The marketing organisation will identify how it wishes to be perceived by the customer and create an environment to reflect this. Public sector organisations may sometimes be constrained in doing this because:

❖ *Many public services face limitations with respect to their location, and in the short term it may be difficult to change the physical environment to reflect the appropriate image.*

❖ *A number of different services may have to share the same premises, and hence there may be a conflict in the image that each service is trying to promote.*

❖ *There are inadequate resources available to create an environment that reflects the desired image.*

## Applying the marketing mix appropriately

As discussed in chapter 3, in order for the marketing strategy to be effectively implemented, the marketing mix has to be correct. The practical application of the marketing mix in the public sector is discussed in the following chapter.

# Summary

❑ Marketing is relevant for all organisations regardless of the sector in which they operate

❑ In the private sector the customer is usually clearly defined. The customer may be an individual or an organisation which is responsible for the use and purchase of the product or service

❑ Users of public sector services are often not responsible for any part of the exchange process and marketing activities need to reflect this

❑ Public and private sectors will use marketing techniques to raise their profiles, demonstrate quality and gain a positive image in the market place

❑ An important step towards successful marketing in the public sector, is to develop a "marketing organisation"

# Exercise 10

## Are You Part of a Marketing Organisation?

| | Score (out of 10) | |
|---|---|---|
| | Yourself Individually | Your Team |
| Professionalism | | |
| Understanding | | |
| Patience | | |
| Enthusiasm | | |
| Acknowledging people | | |
| Friendly and welcoming | | |
| Remembering names | | |
| Using names | | |
| Smiling | | |
| Reassurance | | |
| Confidence | | |
| Open body language | | |
| Checking understanding | | |
| Taking responsibility | | |
| Responding to the customer in a timely fashion: | | |
| - by email | | |
| - by phone | | |
| - by letter | | |
| - by appointment | | |
| - by action | | |
| Handling complaints/blame | | |
| Politeness | | |
| Helpfulness | | |

| | Score (out of 10) | |
|---|---|---|
| | **Yourself Individually** | **Your Team** |
| Appearance | | |
| Listening | | |
| Assertiveness | | |
| Telephone Technique | | |

*Scoring for this exercise can be found on page 123*

# Chapter 6

## PRACTICAL USE OF MARKETING TECHNIQUES

### *Market Research*

This book has emphasised the importance of adequate market research as the cornerstone to the development of a successful marketing strategy. Market research can provide information relating to every facet of the marketing definition, i.e. the identification, anticipation and satisfaction of customer requirements. However, in practice market research can be:

*Time consuming*
*Expensive*
*Inconclusive*

Hence, considerable thought and planning should be applied, particularly in the public sector where resources may be scarce.

The following table sets out some practical suggestions with respect to each area of market research that is commonly used.

# Primary Research (providing original and specific information)

| METHOD | KEY USES | TIPS FOR SUCCESS | PITFALLS TO BEWARE OF |
|---|---|---|---|
| *Written/Postal email/online Questionnaires* | • Collection of quantitative data<br><br>• Establishing key statistics and general trends<br><br>• Gathering large volumes of information<br><br>• Gathering information from a wide range of locations | • Identify key information that needs to be obtained from the research<br><br>• Limit number of questions asked<br><br>• Make questions easy to complete for the target group in question<br><br>• Explain how information obtained will be used<br><br>• Make the majority of questions closed<br><br>• Make response mechanism easy e.g. prepaid envelopes, easy website navigation | • Questionnaires that take more than 10 minutes to complete<br><br>• Questions that have an element of ambiguity<br><br>• Too many open questions that cannot be analysed<br><br>• Poor analysis of results |
| *Verbal/ Telephone Questionnaires* | • Collection of quantitative and qualitative data<br><br>• Establishing key statistics and general trends<br><br>• Gathering large volumes of information<br><br>• Quick way of obtaining feedback<br><br>• Can guarantee a certain number of responses<br><br>• Can ask follow up probing questions depending on the initial response | • Identify key information that needs to be obtained from the research<br><br>• Limit number of questions asked<br><br>• Give a time limit to the interviewee at the outset of the conversation<br><br>• Make the majority of questions closed<br><br>• Explain how information obtained will be used | • Questionnaires that take more than 10 minutes to complete<br><br>• Questions that have an element of ambiguity<br><br>• Too many open and probing questions that cannot be analysed<br><br>• Poor communication skills<br><br>• Insufficient planning in terms of when research is undertaken |

| METHOD | KEY USES | TIPS FOR SUCCESS | PITFALLS TO BEWARE OF |
|---|---|---|---|
| **Focus Groups** | • Collection of qualitative data<br><br>• Establishing specific information relating to specific discussion topics<br><br>• Gathering ideas and opinions<br><br>• Quick way of gathering information from several people at one time<br><br>• Can guarantee a certain level of research and control the number of people involved<br><br>• Can ask follow up probing questions depending on the initial responses | • Identify key information that needs to be obtained from the research<br><br>• Limit number of areas discussed by the group<br><br>• Ensure a skilled group facilitator is used<br><br>• Make the majority of questions open<br><br>• Explain how information obtained will be used<br><br>• Specify the amount of time for each session | • Group facilitators not of a high enough standard<br><br>• High levels of bias arising from responses<br><br>• Inappropriate mix of group participants<br><br>• Inaccurate and/or incomplete note taking<br><br>• Bias in terms of the summary of the discussion |
| **Interviews** | • Collection of qualitative data<br><br>• Establishing individual views on specific topics<br><br>• Gathering ideas and opinions<br><br>• Can guarantee a certain level of research and control the number of people involved<br><br>• Can ask follow up probing questions depending on the initial responses | • Identify key information that needs to be obtained from the research<br><br>• Give interviewee a limited number of areas to discuss<br><br>• Ensure a skilled interviewer is used<br><br>• Make the majority of questions open<br><br>• Explain how information obtained will be used<br><br>• Specify the amount of time for each interview | • Sub-standard interviewing skills<br><br>• Individual bias in some of the responses<br><br>• Weak profiling of interview candidates<br><br>• Poor recording of interview (written or taped) |

| METHOD | KEY USES | TIPS FOR SUCCESS | PITFALLS TO BEWARE OF |
|--------|----------|------------------|------------------------|
| *Observation* | • Collection of quantitative and qualitative data <br><br> • Establishing key statistics and general trends usually about physical/action related topics <br><br> • Gathering large volumes of information <br><br> • Quick way of obtaining information <br><br> • Facts based on actual occurrences | • Identify key information that needs to be obtained from the research <br><br> • Limit number of activities that are being observed at one time <br><br> • Give a time limit to the observation period and inform those being observed that the observation is taking place | • Inconsistent observers <br><br> • Weak or biased interpretation of observations |

Questionnaires are one of the most useful tools when obtaining primary data.

For example, a housing organisation wishes to research the quality of its front of house service, and has decided to produce an online questionnaire for members of the public to complete. The objectives for the questionnaire were identified as follows:

a) To establish the general level of satisfaction with the current reception service

b) To identify areas of improvement that could be implemented (i.e. there are only a limited number of improvements that can be made within the resource constraints and therefore the most popular ones will be chosen for implementation)

c) To establish the current image given by the reception area and to compare that with the image desired by the organisation in the business plan

The questionnaires are to be completed online, and need to be relatively brief, hence the number of questions should be limited such that it takes no more than 5 minutes to complete. The information needs to be easily analysed to give a range of statistics and comparative trends when future questionnaires are performed.

Given the objectives, a possible questionnaire for a reception service is shown as follows:

# Questionnaire for Reception Services

| | | | | |
|---|---|---|---|---|
| 1. How often do you visit the reception? | Weekly ☐ | Monthly ☐ | Very rarely ☐ | |

2. How would you rate the overall reception service?

    Good ☐    Average ☐    Poor ☐

3. How long on average do you wait to be seen? ☐ Minutes

4. Are reception staff polite and helpful?

    Yes ☐    No ☐

5. What image did you develop of the organisation when you first entered reception?

    ☐ Efficient
    ☐ Caring
    ☐ Inefficient
    ☐ Other (please state)
    .........................................

6. Do you think the reception service needs to be improved?

    Yes ☐    No ☐

7. Which of the following improvements do you think would be most beneficial?
   (Select one only, a, b, or c)

   a) Redecoration of the reception area, paint, furniture, etc. ☐
   b) An additional member of staff ☐
   c) An extension of the reception waiting area to include a crèche ☐

8. Are there any other points you would like to make with respect to the reception service?
   .................................................
   .................................................
   .................................................

## Secondary/desk research (providing general information)

This research can provide information about:

- ❖ *Industry trends*
- ❖ *New developments*
- ❖ *Competitors*

The main sources for this data will include:

- ❖ *The internet*
- ❖ *Industry sector publications*
- ❖ *Government statistics and reports*
- ❖ *Magazines and Journals*
- ❖ *Newspapers*
- ❖ *Unpublished data such as research papers, in-house documents, etc.*

To undertake this research successfully, there needs to be a clear allocation of responsibility to allow for the regular review of the internet, articles, taking cuttings/copies of relevant information and keeping a record of this information such that it can be easily retrieved. Where possible, information from the full range of sources should be linked and collated by subject matter such that it can be used in the development of the marketing strategy.

# *Application of the Marketing Mix*

The relevance of each element of the marketing mix will vary depending on the nature of the organisation, and its market place. For example, in the public sector, price may be a less important element of the mix as many services are not directly charged for, whereas location and access may be very important.

The following diagram sets out five simple questions in respect of each element of the marketing mix. The answers will assist an organisation to identify the relative importance of each element and how they should be balanced with each other in a practical way.

## Product/Service

- Why do customers use the service?
- Does it meet customer requirements?
- What continuous improvements can be made?
- Is it provided by other organisations and if so how does it compare?
- What is the desired relative quality level compared to the market in general, and are those levels being achieved?

## Place/Distribution

- Is the service accessible to those who require it?
- Is information about the service accessible to those who need to know about it?
- Is the service delivered on time?
- Is the service adequately supported?
- Does the place or distribution method reflect the image of the organisation?

## People
Customers
Users
Staff
Stakeholders
General Public

## Promotion

- What are the key messages that need to be communicated about the service?
- Who needs to receive the communication? (See range of people)
- What media is available to send the relevant communication?
- What resources are available for promotional activities?
- How is the success of promotional activities going to be measured?

## Price

- Is the service competitively priced compared to other similar services in the market?
- Is the price higher than the cost?
- How do purchasers perceive the price? (expensive, cheap, good value, etc.)
- Can the price be easily changed, and is it possible to offer price incentives? (special offers, discounts, etc.)

# *Public Relations*

Public Relations (PR) is one aspect of promotion which is very important to the public sector and can prove very costly if the incorrect approach is taken. PR can either be conducted in-house or by an external consultancy or using a combination of both. The decision as to which approach is adopted will depend on:

❖ *The size of the organisation*

❖ *The importance placed on PR and image*

❖ *The available budget*

❖ *The in-house skills available*


There are advantages and dis-advantages to both approaches

| In-house PR | External PR |
|---|---|
| **→ *Advantages*** | **→ *Advantages*** |
| • Have a full time service that can react quickly (particularly useful in the public sector if a serious problem arises that needs a quick response, e.g. health scares) | • Wide range of experience and expertise available to be applied to each situation |
| • Fixed cost, being mainly staff salaries | • Flexibility and choice as more than one PR consultancy may be engaged for different areas, and services can easily be terminated if unsatisfactory |
| • Control over the way in which PR is handled across the whole organisation, particularly the media | • Independence and objectivity |
| • In-depth knowledge of the organisation and its philosophies | • Can be cost effective, as only used when required. This is particularly the case if PR activities are only undertaken on an adhoc basis |
| • No conflict of interest | |

| In-house PR | External PR |
|---|---|
| **→ Disadvantages** | **→ Disadvantages** |
| • Lack of experience and expertise available within a small team | • Possible conflicts of interest as a consultancy may have many different clients on its books |
| • Lack of innovation and ideas, especially where staff remain in position for a long time with only the one organisation to work with | • May be very expensive |
| • Lack of objectivity | • Potential lack of in-depth knowledge of the organisation due to the slightly arms length relationship |
| • May be costly if not fully utilised all the time | |

The main PR activities usually undertaken in the public sector include:

❖ *Press, television and radio releases*

❖ *Website news and information*

❖ *Internet networking such as Twitter, Facebook, etc.*

❖ *Public appearances*

❖ *Seminars and conferences*

❖ *Influencing strategic people and organisations (e.g. lobbying)*

Effective PR requires a range of different skills and hence it is quite common to have a mixture of both in-house and external PR systems in operation.

# *Relevance of Selling*

The income of most private companies is derived by the selling of their products or services directly to customers. The sale is the exchange of the product or service usually for cash or a cash equivalent. Therefore, these companies will set sales targets, and will have developed an approach to selling appropriate to their product/service and customers.

For many public sector organisations, the majority of income is derived from some form of grant originating from public funds, with other sources of income including rents, interest, donations, fees and charges. In many cases, very little income is derived from actual sales of services and hence selling may not be perceived to be a key issue. However, where sales do represent an important source of income, the organisation should approach selling in a professional and methodical manner. This entails:

❖ *Identifying key personnel responsible for sales (these sales staff may be fully or partly involved in this activity depending on the volumes concerned)*

❖ *Ensuring sales staff have appropriate sales training*

❖ *Developing a sales strategy based on sales objectives (e.g. having different approaches and targets for different customer types, different regions, etc.)*

❖ *Ensuring a high level of product/service knowledge amongst sales staff*

❖ *Ensuring consistency in the way in which sales staff communicate with customers*

❖ *Having an agreed pricing policy such that staff know the amount of flexibility they have with respect to negotiating prices, if at all*

❖ *Establishing weekly or monthly sales targets which have to be met*

❖ *Ensuring that production/provider departments are able to support sales (i.e. deliver what has been sold)*

The public sector can also adopt some of the same selling techniques which exist in the private sector. These include:

❖ *Email marketing*

❖ *Telesales*

❖ *Personal contact*

❖ *Presentations*

❖ *Demonstrations*

❖ *Promotions and special offers*

❖ *Advertising*

❖ *Direct mail*

The main prohibiting factor to the implementation of some of these techniques may be cost relative to the amount of potential sales income generated.

## *Internal Marketing*

In many large organisations, the work of some departments will be to support the service provided by other departments, this is especially the case in the public sector. As part of the development of public sector services, there has been a drive to ensure that all parts of the organisation are cost effective and provide best value for money. Hence, in some cases, an internal market has been developed for those supplying support services. This means that where customer departments are part of the same organisation, support service departments need to have an internal marketing strategy.

In such cases all the same principles of marketing apply. For example:

❖ *Finding out what the customer requires using market research techniques*

❖ *Developing the product and service to meet customer requirements*

❖ *Ensuring the service is accessible*

❖ *Promoting the service*

❖ *Maximising customer satisfaction*

The internal market place may be very complex, particularly with respect to the way in which in-house services are financed. Some organisations establish a trading like environment, for example, schools purchasing services from the local authority, or a housing department purchasing legal advice from the legal services department. This type of arrangement requires the support service department to generate sufficient income from internal customers to cover its costs. In such circumstances, an effective marketing strategy may be essential to the survival of the in-house service. Insufficient internal customers may lead to the service being contracted out either to the private sector or to an alternative public or third sector supplier. Common examples of this have been in the area of payroll services, elements of legal services, and training.

# Summary

❑ Questionnaires are one of the most useful tools when obtaining primary data

❑ Secondary desk research can be used to provide information about industry trends, new developments and competitors. This information can be obtained from a variety of sources including the internet, industry sector publications, government statistics, reports, magazines and journals

❑ PR is one aspect of promotion which is very important to the public sector and can prove very costly if the incorrect approach is taken. PR can either be conducted by an external consultancy or in-house, or a combination of both

❑ Where a public sector organisation sells some of its services/products and these sales represent an important source of income, it should approach selling in a professional manner and may even adopt some of the same techniques which exist in the private sector

# Exercise 11

## Implementing the Marketing Plan

The Pine Valley National Park Authority has developed a marketing strategy and marketing plan with the aid of a consultant and is now deciding whether or not to undertake marketing in-house or to engage one or more consultancies. The manager responsible has the following three options:

### Option 1

*To deliver the marketing plan, 3 members of staff would be needed as follows:*

| | |
|---|---|
| *Promotions Officer* | *£22,000* |
| *PR Officer* | *£25,000* |
| *Advertising Officer* | *£24,000* |

*In addition, overheads will be required, including accommodation, computers, etc. In total this will be £14,000. Given the activities required there is a possibility of making the PR officer position part-time, but by having a full time person there will be scope for the person to undertake in-house design projects and give advice to managers on internal communication, (this work could be charged to departments generating £5,000 per annum). All employees would be expected to work the necessary hours in order to complete important projects and overtime would not be paid.*

### Option 2

*A PR consultancy could be retained for the year at £30,000. This would cover all the projects identified in the marketing plan and any additional work that comes up would be charged at £120 per hour. In addition, an advertising agency would be needed requiring a retainer of £20,000 per year and a charge of £150 per hour for additional work. A marketing consultant would also be engaged requiring a £32,000 retainer per year. The consultant is prepared to undertake additional work without extra charge within reason, i.e. up to 12 hours but would be unlikely to be able to fit in any further work.*

## Option 3
*A quote received from a large marketing consultancy that could offer a complete service for £80,000 for the year to deliver all aspects of the marketing plan; but would be charging £140 per hour for any additional work.*

Even though the marketing plan has been thoughtfully developed, the manager considers it prudent to expect at least 2 additional PR projects at an estimated 10 hours each, 1 advertising project at an estimated 5 hours and 1 additional promotions initiative at an estimated 12 hours.

*Note: It is assumed that the direct costs incurred will be the same in all cases (e.g. email marketing, printing leaflets, placing advertisements, room hire, refreshments, etc.)*

## *You are the consultant.*
## *Justify your advice in financial terms*

*For suggested solutions to this exercise see page 124*

# Exercise 12

## Action Plan

List the practical actions you intend to take over the next 12 months to achieve your marketing objectives.

| Marketing Objectives |
|---|
|  |

| Actions | Timescale | Person responsible |
|---|---|---|
|  |  |  |
|  |  |  |
|  |  |  |
|  |  |  |
|  |  |  |

| Actions | Timescale | Person responsible |
|---------|-----------|--------------------|
|         |           |                    |
|         |           |                    |
|         |           |                    |
|         |           |                    |
|         |           |                    |
|         |           |                    |
|         |           |                    |
|         |           |                    |
|         |           |                    |
|         |           |                    |

# Chapter 7

## MARKETING CASE STUDIES

This section sets out a number of case studies showing how marketing techniques can be applied within public sector organisations.

### Case Study 1
*"Marketing Without a Budget"*

### Poortown Secondary School

Schools are currently being judged by their league table success identifying how well students are performing in examinations. These tables are used by parents in assessing their choice of school. As school funding is partly based on pupil numbers, it is important to ensure that each year the school operates at full capacity.

Poortown Secondary School has recently performed very badly in the league tables, and has developed a poor reputation in the local area because of the behavioural problems of some of its pupils. This has resulted in falling pupil numbers for the last few years, and it is critical that this trend is reversed for the long term survival of the school. This year a new Head Teacher has been appointed and some dramatic changes are going to take place which should improve performance. One of the first tasks of the new head was to develop a marketing strategy that would change the image of the school and reverse the trend of falling pupil numbers.

The new Head has many innovative ideas, but was informed that there was no budget available to implement a marketing plan, and therefore, had to adopt a marketing strategy based on the following factors:

## Objective:

To change Poortown's image and encourage more parents to send their children.

## Market Place:

A number of other schools in the local and neighbouring areas are currently more successful and more popular

## Target Groups:

Parents, children and the local authority

## Competitive Advantages:

New head with an excellent track record, new approach to discipline, new approach to teacher *recruitment and training, open and communicative style with parents*

## *Marketing Mix:*

*Product* – *Strive towards excellence in the quality of the education service delivered, improve performance in league tables, widen range of options available within the scope of the curriculum, increase the number of after school activities*

*Place* – *Improvements to school premises, more open day activities to include parents*

*Promotion* – *Educate parents about the changes; update the website; encourage parents to see the school for themselves; talk to teachers and the head; create a positive image with success stories, and promote word of mouth propaganda*

The actions required for the marketing plan had to be zero cost and were designed as follows:

■  Change the atmosphere within the school to one where hard work, performance and discipline are the only acceptable behaviours. This is to be led from the top by the head and followed through by teachers. Aids to implementation were:

- Development of a mission statement which formed a common identity across the school

- Training courses in class control, communication, etc.

- Teacher image and presentation

- Frequent open days, awards, etc. to instil pride in the school and it's performance

- New and publicised code of conduct, along with a new range of disciplinary actions involving parents, all of which promoted on the website

■ Additional classes for students who need help to reach higher standards of performance, by obtaining the goodwill of staff to assist on a voluntary basis

■ Increased correspondence with existing parents highlighting successes, and promoting the philosophy of the new Head

■ Activities to help the local community, such as environmental projects, helping older people, events, etc.

■ Publication of a regular monthly school news bulletin, emphasising positive aspects of the school, produced by students and distributed to parents, pupils, governors, and the local community by way of email, and highlighted on the home page of the website

- Development of a prospectus produced by staff and students and given to all those who enquire about the school

The Head is aware that all the activities will have to be undertaken in-house and will rely on the goodwill and support of the existing staff and parents to assist in implementing the action plan. It is expected that continued effort of the kind identified above will achieve the objective over a three year period, when the outcomes of the marketing plan will be assessed.

### Case Study 2
*"Measuring Marketing Success"*

## Social Services Department - Niceleigh County Council (NCC)

NCC social services department have been implementing a marketing plan over the past three years. The marketing plan was developed by the department with the assistance of external consultants, and initially cost £10,000. Implementation costs over the last three years have averaged £32,000 per annum and have included a new corporate image and logo, updated website, printed information, leaflets, publicity advertisements in local papers and on radio stations, review of current service provision, and training for staff, regular internal and external newsletters and so on.

The managers of NCC social services consider the marketing plan has been a success and has achieved the original objectives which were:

1. *To raise the profile of the key services provided by the department in the eyes of councillors, staff, users and the general public*

2. *In order to increase usage and fee income, to promote specific revenue producing services such as the panic alarm service*

3. *To educate users and the public regarding the range of services on offer*

4. *To increase the level of customer satisfaction, and reduce complaints across the department*

5. *To demonstrate that the department provides best value for money in all its activities*

The Chief Executive now requires the department to produce a report showing tangible evidence the investment in marketing has been justified.

In order to prepare the report, the following activities were undertaken:

a) **Identifying the cost of the marketing effort**, including staff time spent on marketing activities, and

b) **Identifying the starting position for each of the objectives** and comparing them with the current position, and where possible placing a monetary value on the change

### *a) Identifying the cost*

| | £ |
|---|---|
| Initial consultancy | 10,000 |
| Consultant reviews | 6,000 |
| 3 years implementation | 96,000 |
| Staff time, one full time equivalent officer each year | 63,000 |
| Administration | 15,000 |
| Postage, stationery, etc. | 21,000 |
| Management time | 9,000 |
| **TOTAL** | **220,000** |

## b) Three year progress comparison

| Obj | Original Position | Current Position | Change |
|---|---|---|---|
| 1 | A poor profile across the department generally and therefore the department was assumed to have low quality services, inefficient staff, etc. | A positive image amongst all concerned resulting in commendations and high levels of support from Council members, staff, users, and the local community | Difficult to tie in value with the marketing effort, but clearly marketing had a positive impact. Increased value of legacies each year to an average of £27,000. Lower staff turnover saving in recruitment costs value £12,000 |
| 2 | Revenue producing services netted a total income after costs of £50,000 per annum | Net income increased by in excess of 20% year on year and are currently £90,000 | Total increased revenues over the three year period values £70,000 |
| 3 | A great deal of staff time was spent explaining services to callers and visitors, along with dissatisfaction arising when users were not able to receive the services they wanted | A reduction in general enquiries by 25% due to the availability of comprehensive information on the website, and regular emails which are pro-actively sent to potential service users, along with easy to read leaflets available in libraries etc. Also less dissatisfaction as available service provision is known in advance | Reduction in enquiries represents a saving in staff time which manifested itself in the saving of one identified salary. Many staff benefited because they had more time to spend on other aspects of the service. Identified saving, £38,000. |

| Obj | Original Position | Current Position | Change |
|-----|-------------------|------------------|--------|
| 4 | A survey undertaken had overall satisfaction as 58% | Most recent survey had satisfaction as 82% | Increased satisfaction has resulted in higher morale, more time spent on service delivery as opposed to dealing with dissatisfied customers. Difficult to put a value on the change as the systems to record staff time were not in place at the outset |
| 5 | Complaints averaged 5 minor ones per week and one major one per month | Complaints currently average 2 minor ones per week and 4 major ones per year | The significant reduction in complaints is closely related to the increase in satisfaction. Each complaint requires the complaints procedure to be undertaken which has been costed at an average of £100 per minor complaint and £2,000 per major complaint. Hence, the estimated value in savings £84,000 |
| 6 | Unit costs for some of the department's activities that could be compared with other providers, appeared substantially higher in almost all areas, some as much as 100% higher | Unit costs of the same activities are now competitive compared to other providers with none being more than 20% higher | The reduced unit costs have been largely achieved by increasing productivity, although some genuine savings have been made. |

With this information, the department was able to report that the marketing plan achieved more than a "feel good" factor, but had resulted in tangible results which showed the investment was surpassed by gains in monetary terms which totalled £231,000 compared with the cost of £220,000. It is clear from the described changes that even greater benefits were achieved as a result of the marketing effort and other tangible statistics were used in the report including:

- *Reduced staff turnover*

- *Reduced absence*

- *Increases in customer satisfaction*

- *Reductions in complaints*

- *Increased income*

- *Reduced unit costs*

Although the results proved positive, the department realised that they were not able to really measure the extent of their successes because there were no targets set with respect to the original objectives. Hence, the department does not know whether or not they have exceeded what would have been realistic expectations. This has been rectified with respect to the marketing plan for the next three year period.

### Case Study 3
*"A Truly Marketing Organisation"*

## Bentonville General Hospital (BGH)

Given all the changes to the health service and the establishment of a market place for state health care, BGH decided to take the opportunity to change and develop the hospital into a truly market oriented establishment. This would mean the customer would become the central focus of all activities undertaken by the hospital.

To begin with there was considerable resistance to the idea, particularly from senior management on the grounds of cost, and from staff on the grounds of additional work. However, after the Chief Executive explained the benefits of the change, a commitment was made to implement a five year action plan which is currently being introduced.

The action plan was broken down into key areas as follows:

### Services

- Continued service development based on user feedback from questionnaires, focus groups and one to one interviews

- Innovative approaches to existing services arising from staff and user suggestions which are pro-actively sought

- Access to services made user friendly

- Educate users about the available services, and the way in which they are delivered.

Questions from users are encouraged and all activities undertaken are fully explained

### *Staff*

- In depth training in customer care

- In depth training in communication (face to face and over the telephone)

- Development of staff attitudes emphasising the need to put customer's first

- Regular staff briefings so that all staff are up to date with the services offered, and are able to speak confidently to users

- Integration of professional and administrative staff to encourage the development of a seamless service

- Appraisal schemes which identify staff who are not customer oriented and take action to either change or remove those individuals

### *Users*

- Increased levels of information

- Increased participation in decision making as to how services should be delivered

- Surveys with respect to current services, changes, new services, the environment and the infrastructure

- Regular communication with users, particularly those who have had to spend a length of time in the hospital

Regular progress reports are made and published for all interested parties to read and comment upon. Becoming a marketing organisation will not be a quick process, but BGH are at least attempting to achieve that goal.

# SOLUTIONS TO EXERCISES

# Solutions to Exercises

# Solution to Exercise 2
## Assessing the Service/Product

Award 2 points for every "yes" ticked and 0 points for every "no" ticked and add the total points. Your resulting score is summarised as follows:

### 0 to 12

The current product/service is not satisfactory, and there is insufficient knowledge of either the market place or customers in order to develop a satisfactory service. It is suggested that some market research and considerable service development be undertaken before attempting to look at the other aspects of the marketing mix.

### 14 to 26

This is an average score and the one most likely to be achieved by most organisations. It is clear that some thought has been given to the type of product/service being delivered, but there is room for considerable improvement. The aim should be to answer all the questions positively, therefore, take the necessary actions needed to turn each of the "no" answers into a "yes".

### 28 to 40

This score shows that you have an excellent service which meets customer requirements, and that is continuously developed to meet changing needs. If the score was not perfect there are still a few actions that can be taken to further improve the service. Continue in the same way.

# Solution to Exercise 10
## Are You Part of a Marketing Organisation?

**Scores below 150** demonstrate very poor performance in relation to the ideal marketing organisation and therefore a lot of work should be put into developing good customer care practice. If your personal score is at this level then training in all aspects of marketing is essential. If this is a team score, then training is required for the whole team, in addition to a general review of working practices along with the development of appropriate management policies such as customer care.

**Scores between 150 and 200** reflect an adequate level of attention to customers but indicate that there is room for improvement. If this is your personal score, it is clear that you are aware of the customer and have the right ideas as to how customers should be treated, however, it is not consistent throughout the whole process of dealing with the customer. If this is the score for your team, there is still a need for training for all staff in order to develop the organisation to understand that marketing is part of the management process which particularly manifests itself in the way in which customers are treated.

**Scores in excess of 200** demonstrates that many of the factors needed to be a marketing organisation are already in place in so far as the approach taken by you and/or your team puts a high emphasis on good customer relations. This level needs to be maintained and monitored. Performance indicators should show low levels of customer complaint, high levels of customer satisfaction and high staff morale.

# Solution to Exercise 11
## Implementing the Marketing Plan

As stated in chapter 6, there are advantages and disadvantages to all the options, therefore this solution only takes into account the financial implications set out in the example. In a real life situation, issues other than finance may take priority.

### *Calculating the Costs*

*Option 1 ~ In-house Provision:*

|  | £ |
|---|---|
| Salaries | 71,000 |
| Overheads | 14,000 |
| Advice/Design | (5,000) * |
| **TOTAL** | **80,000** |

* *Note: this is a notional saving, not necessarily recoverable in monetary terms. Therefore, the cash outlay represented in the budget would be considered to be £85,000.*

*Option 2 ~ Mix of three different consultants:*

|  | £ |
|---|---|
| PR consultancy retainer | 30,000 |
| Additional projects (20 hours @ £120) | 2,400 |
| Advertising agency retainer | 20,000 |
| Additional projects (5 hours @ £150) | 750 |
| Marketing consultant | 32,000 |
| **TOTAL** | **85,150** |

## Option 3 ~ Marketing Consultancy

| | £ |
|---|---:|
| Marketing consultancy for complete service | 80,000 |
| Additional projects & promotions | |
| (37 hours @ £140) | <u>5,180</u> |
| **TOTAL** | **<u>85,180</u>** |

All the above costs are very similar, however, in the case of option 2, the marketing consultant may not be able to deliver the service required if the full 12 hours of additional work needs to be undertaken. However, without the contingency for additional work, both options 2 and 3 would be cheaper than the in-house option.

The prudent approach would be to take account of the expected additional work and hence on this basis the manager should select option 1.

# INDEX

# A

# B

# C

# G

Government policies · 79
Government statistics · 93
Grant · 98

# I

Image · 24, 52, 71, 82
Implementing the Marketing Plan · 54
Income · 98
Industry sector · 93
Industry trends · 93
In-house services · 100
Inputs to the service · 21
Interest · 98
Internal market · 46
Internal marketing · 99
International market · 46

# J

Journals · 93

# L

Legislation · 69, 79
Local market · 46

# M

Magazines · 93
Management · 6
Management style · 81
Market economy · 5
Market environment · 52
Market place · 74
Market place map · 67
Market place stability · 47

# N

# O

# P

# Q

# R

---

# U

---

# V

---

# W

For further information see www.hbpublications.com
and www.fci-system.com